Southern
Cookbook

Barbara Bloch

ILLUSTRATED BY
PATRICIA AND
ROBIN DE WITT

First published in 1991 by
The Appletree Press Ltd, 7 James Street South,
Belfast BT2 8DL.
© 1991 The Appletree Press Ltd.
Illustrations © 1991 Patricia and Robin DeWitt
used under Exclusive License to
The Appletree Press Ltd.
Printed in Hong Kong. All rights reserved.
No part of this publication may be
reproduced or transmitted in any form or by
any means, electronic or mechanical,
photocopying, recording or any information
and retrieval system, without permission in
writing from the publisher.

First published in the United States in 1991
by Chronicle Books, 275 Fifth Street,
San Francisco, CA 94103.

ISBN: 0-87701-877-4

9 8 7 6 5 4 3 2 1

Introduction

Although I was born and raised in the North, the food I ate as a child included the southern dishes my grandmother served — Baking Powder Biscuits, Crab Meat Aspic, Fig Preserves, Fried Chicken, and Grits, one of my father's favorite foods. The southerner I married has a similar fondness for Grits and a passion for Guava Jelly, Southern Pot Roast, Pompano, Shad Roe, and almost any fish he can catch. Southern cooking is a varied, ever-changing cuisine. It reflects the food preferences of early European settlers, the cooking talents of the African slaves, the food indigenous to the climate, and soul food, the food of impoverished slaves from the rural South.

A note on measures
Spoon and dry cup measurements are level. Seasonings can of course be adjusted according to taste. Recipes are for four unless otherwise indicated.

Sliced Ham with Red-Eye Gravy

A traditional southern breakfast, which is probably a "sometimes thing" in these modern days of rushing to work and school, can consist of all kinds of food — grits, biscuits, sausage, steak, fish, potatoes, eggs, as well as juice, fruit, coffee, and Sliced Ham with Red-Eye Gravy. By present standards, this dish may not be the healthiest thing to eat, but it remains popular, particularly for those who face a day of heavy physical labor.

---

4 slices, cured country ham, $1/4$-inch thick
about 1 cup hot black coffee

Trim fat from slices of ham and cut fat into small pieces. Place fat in skillet and cook until rendered. Discard pieces of crisp fat and fry ham slices in skillet until browned on both sides. Remove ham to serving dishes and keep warm. Pour coffee into skillet over high heat and deglaze pan, scraping up particles in pan with wooden spoon. Pour over ham and serve with eggs, grits, homemade biscuits, and strong hot coffee.

Baked Cheese and Grits Casserole

It was President Carter who made grits famous. I suspect many northerners had never heard of grits before he became president. Grits is one of those foods most southerners consider a staple and most northerners wouldn't be caught dead eating. My husband likes plain grits, seasoned with butter, salt, and pepper, as an accompaniment to fish. My father preferred plain grits too, but he ate them for breakfast. I like them best as a side dish with a boost from extra flavoring such as cheese and garlic.

1/2 cup milk
1 egg
1 cup grits (cooked according to pkg directions)
8 oz Cheddar cheese, grated
4 tbsp butter
1 or 2 cloves garlic, minced (optional)
salt and freshly ground pepper to taste
paprika
(serves 6)

Preheat oven to 350°F. Grease 2-quart casserole. Beat milk and egg and stir into cooked grits. Set aside 4 tbsp grated cheese. Stir in remaining cheese, butter, garlic, salt, and pepper. Spoon into prepared casserole dish and smooth top. Sprinkle with reserved cheese and paprika. Bake 30 minutes.

Orange-Pecan Bread

Combine the flavors of two of the largest and most popular southern crops to make this delicious quick bread.

---

2 cups all-purpose flour
$1/2$ cup firmly packed brown sugar
$1/2$ cup granulated sugar
1 tsp baking powder
1 tsp baking soda
$1/2$ tsp salt
1 cup coarsely chopped pecans
1 tbsp grated orange peel
1 cup fresh orange juice
1 egg, beaten
3 tbsp vegetable oil

Preheat oven to 350°F. Grease 9- x 5-inch loaf pan. Sift first 6 ingredients into mixing bowl. Stir in pecans and orange peel. Combine orange juice, egg, and vegetable oil in a large cup measure and beat until thoroughly blended. Add to dry ingredients, stirring just until moistened. Pour batter into loaf pan and bake 60 minutes or until cake tester comes out clean. Cool in pan on wire rack 10 minutes. Remove bread from pan and cool completely on rack. Slice when cool.

Buttermilk or Baking Powder Biscuits

My grandmother was forty years old before circumstances required that she learn how to cook. She never became a great cook — or even a very good cook — but she certainly could make a "mean" biscuit.

---

2 cups all-purpose flour
2 tsp baking powder
$^1/_4$ tsp baking soda
$^1/_2$ tsp salt
5 tbsp shortening
$^3/_4$ cup buttermilk

Preheat oven to 450°F. Sift dry ingredients into bowl. Cut in shortening with pastry blender or 2 knives until mixture resembles coarse crumbs. Add buttermilk and stir vigorously to make smooth dough. Place dough on lightly floured surface and knead about 10 times. Roll out dough to $^1/_2$ inch thickness. Cut into rounds by pressing straight down with floured 2 inch biscuit cutter. Place biscuits $^1/_2$ inch apart on ungreased baking sheet. Bake 12 to 14 minutes or until golden. Remove from baking sheet immediately and serve hot.

Baking Powder Biscuits
Substitute whole milk for buttermilk, omit baking soda, and increase baking powder to 1 tbsp.

Mississippi Fig Preserves

The best Fig Preserves I ever ate were made with figs that grew in the backyard of a family home in Starkville, Mississippi. After my grandmother moved north, her niece sent her homemade Fig Preserves every year. Grandmother hid them in her closet and doled them out slowly, determined to make them last all year. She served them with Baking Powder Biscuits, allocating a few figs to each member of the family except my father, who would have been allowed to eat an entire jar, had he been so inclined. Those figs were, quite literally, the forbidden fruit of my youth.

---

*2 to 2 1/2 lbs (about 24) firm, fresh figs (Brown Turkey Figs
preferred, but other kinds may be used)
3 1/2 cups sugar
I lemon, sliced and pits removed*

Rinse figs thoroughly under cold running water. Place sugar in heavy saucepan, and add 3 cups water. Bring to a boil and cook, stirring, until sugar is dissolved. Add figs and lemon slices and cook 25 to 30 minutes or until figs are almost translucent. Stir figs occasionally to prevent them from sticking and add small amounts of additional water during cooking if syrup gets too thick. Cool overnight. Place figs and syrup in hot, sterilized jars. Process 30 minutes in hot-water bath. Refrigerate any extra syrup and use on pancakes or waffles.

Crab Meat Aspic

Although this aspic can be served many ways, for some unknown reason, my grandmother only served it with Chicken Gumbo. It's an ideal luncheon dish for a hot summer day, an elegant addition to a buffet table, and a delicious first course for a company dinner.

---

2 pkgs (I oz each) unflavored gelatin
$1/2$ cup cold tomato juice
$3 1/4$ cups boiling tomato juice
$1/4$ cup lemon juice
hot pepper sauce and salt to taste
I lb crab meat, picked over and flaked
2 stalks celery, diced
lettuce to garnish and mayonnaise to serve
(serves 8)

Place gelatin in medium-size bowl. Stir in cold tomato juice to soften. Add hot tomato juice and stir until gelatin is completely dissolved. Stir in lemon juice, hot pepper sauce, and salt. Set aside until cool and slightly thickened. Fold in crab meat and celery. Rinse 6-cup mold in cold water. Pour aspic into mold and place in refrigerator several hours or until set. When ready to serve, unmold onto serving plate, surround with lettuce, and serve with mayonnaise.

Avocado and Fruit Salad

Avocado salad can be simply a ripe avocado half with vinaigrette dressing. To make a more elegant salad, fill avocado halves with crab meat, shrimp, or chicken salad. Diced or sliced avocado can be added to many salads and, when it is combined with fruit, the result is a light, refreshing combination of flavors.

Dressing
1/2 cup mayonnaise
1/4 cup dairy sour cream
2 tbsp honey
salt and freshly ground white pepper to taste
Salad
lettuce
2 medium-size avocados, peeled, pitted, and sliced
lime or lemon juice
l large grapefruit, peeled and sectioned
mint leaves or parsley sprigs to garnish
(serves 6)

Place dressing ingredients in bowl and beat gently to combine. Arrange lettuce on salad plates. Sprinkle sliced avocados with lime juice and arrange on lettuce with grapefruit sections. Spoon dressing over and garnish with mint leaves.

Goober Soup

Goobers is another name for peanuts — but peanuts aren't nuts at all, they're legumes because they grow underground! They made their way to America on slave ships and are an integral part of African cooking. Goober Soup dates back to colonial times, but it wasn't until after the Civil War that peanuts really took off when Dr. George Washington Carver made them famous. Modern soup recipes use peanut butter, something that wasn't available until 1904.

---

4 tbsp butter
I small onion
I stalk celery, chopped
4 tbsp all-purpose flour
3 cups chicken stock
I cup creamy peanut butter
3 cups milk or light cream
$1/8$ tsp each ground ginger and cloves
salt and freshly ground pepper to taste
4 tbsp chopped peanuts to garnish

Melt butter in large saucepan. Add onion and celery and sauté until softened. Stir in flour and cook 2 minutes. Stir in chicken stock slowly and simmer 30 minutes. Pour into food processor or blender and purée. Return to saucepan. Place peanut butter in bowl and stir in milk slowly. Add to saucepan. Season and simmer until thickened and heated through. Garnish each serving with I tbsp chopped peanuts.

Crab-Corn Chowder

Blue crabs, found all along the Atlantic, are particularly abundant in the Gulf of Mexico. I can't help but wonder what my great-grandfather must have thought the first time he ate them, having come to Mobile, Alabama in 1848 from inland Europe. Crab meat can be used in all kinds of recipes, and soup that includes crab meat can be a festive way to start a meal.

---

3 tbsp butter
1 small onion, finely chopped
1 small green pepper, finely chopped
3 tbsp all-purpose flour
2 cups chicken stock
2 cups half and half or light cream
cayenne and salt to taste
1 pkg (10 oz) frozen whole-kernel corn, thawed
8 oz crab meat
freshly chopped parsley to garnish

Melt butter in large saucepan. Add onion and green pepper and sauté just until softened. Stir in flour and cook 3 minutes. Add chicken stock and cream slowly, stirring constantly. Add corn and crab meat, season, and cook over low heat, stirring, until mixture is thickened. Simmer 10 minutes. Adjust seasoning and spoon into small soup bowls. Garnish with parsley.

Southern Fried Chicken

You have to have been born in the South to make really good fried chicken! I'm convinced it's a matter of genes. My knowledge of cooking and southern heritage don't help one bit. My husband makes better fried chicken than I do. Southern cooks all have their own recipes, and recipes vary dramatically from one state to the next. We like this recipe because it's ideal picnic food, and we can even take it on a trip when the prospect of having nothing to eat but airplane food takes the appetite away.

---

2 broiler/fryer chickens (about 4 lb each), cut up
all-purpose flour seasoned with cayenne, paprika, salt, and freshly ground pepper
4 eggs, beaten with $1/2$ tsp vegetable oil
seasoned cracker meal (see flour above)
vegetable oil for cooking
(serves 6)

Coat chicken with seasoned flour, dip in beaten eggs, and coat with seasoned cracker meal. Heat oil in 2 heavy skillets. Place dark meat, skin side down, in first skillet and white meat, skin side down, in second skillet. Cook slowly over moderate heat until well browned and tender, turning chicken with tongs. Dark meat will take about 45 minutes to cook, white meat about 30 minutes. Drain on paper towels. Serve hot or at room temperature.

Baked Virginia or Smithfield Ham

Virginia or Smithfield Ham is one of the South's true culinary treasures. Its one disadvantage is that preparation can't be hurried. Many people prefer to buy cooked ham, expensive as it is, because otherwise it must be soaked 12 to 24 hours, and the smallest ham (about 10 lb) takes at least 5 hours to cook.

---

1 Virginia or Smithfield Ham, 10 to 14 lb
about 50 whole cloves
1 cup firmly packed brown sugar
$1/2$ cup honey
2 tbsp prepared mustard
(serves 25 to 30)

Place ham in large pot or roasting pan, cover with water, and soak 12 to 24 hours, changing water frequently to remove excess salt. Drain ham and scrape off mold. Preheat oven to 300°F. Place ham in roasting pan, add 10 cups water, and cover pan with aluminum foil. Bake 20 to 25 minutes per lb. Remove ham from oven, leaving oven on. Remove skin, score ham, and stud with cloves. Place sugar, honey, and mustard in small bowl and stir to combine. Spread over ham. Drain pan and place ham on rack in roasting pan. Bake, uncovered, 30 minutes. For added flavor, baste ham with bourbon during final baking. Slice ham paper-thin and serve hot or cold.

Southern Pot Roast

This recipe was given to me by my husband when we were first married. It's a family favorite from his childhood. He insists it absolutely must be served with hot (spicy) chow-chow pickles, and we even have a special dish in which his mother always served them.

---

4 lb boneless beef bottom or top round roast
2 cups beef stock
1 can (16 oz) stewed tomatoes
1 can (16 oz) tomato sauce
1 large onion, 1 green pepper and
1 stalk celery, chopped
2 cloves garlic, minced
1 teaspoon sugar
salt and freshly ground pepper to taste
8 medium-size potatoes, peeled, cut in half, and cooked
8 carrots, cut into 2-inch chunks and cooked
16 small white onions, cooked
hot chow-chow pickles to serve
(serves 8)

Brown meat on all sides under broiler. Place remaining ingredients, except cooked vegetables, in large saucepan. Add meat, bring to a boil, skim off fat, reduce heat, cover, and simmer 3 1/2 hours or until very tender. Turn meat several times during cooking, adding additional stock or water if necessary. Remove meat to carving board and slice. Taste sauce and adjust seasoning. Surround sliced meat with hot vegetables and spoon sauce over. Serve with chow-chow pickles.

Texas Barbecued Steak

The language keeps changing, and the way we use the word "barbecue" is no exception. Time was when barbecue was a noun as in "let's have a barbecue." It also was a verb as in "it's time to barbecue the food." But these days it's not uncommon to hear people say they "ate a barbecue," leaving me to wonder if they had eaten the cooking equipment on the terrace. This language change from the South doesn't detract from the fact that barbecued food is always a treat.

---

1 1/2 cups vegetable oil
3/4 cup soy sauce
1/2 cup red wine vinegar
1/4 cup Worcestershire sauce
2 cloves garlic, crushed
2 tbsp dry mustard dissolved in small amount of water
chili powder, cumin, and freshly ground pepper to taste
2 1/2 lb beef round top round steak, cut 2-inches thick
hot chili sauce to serve
(serves 4 to 6)

Place all ingredients except meat in blender and process until thoroughly combined. Place meat in glass or china baking dish and pierce on both sides in several places with fork. Pour sauce over, cover, and refrigerate at least 4 hours. Turn meat over 3 or 4 times during refrigeration. Preheat grill and cook meat to desired doneness, basting with sauce several times during cooking. Slice against grain and serve immediately with hot chili sauce.

Sautéed Pompano

If you're anywhere near the Gulf of Mexico, or along the southern Atlantic coast, you can find freshly caught pompano in season. If you're elsewhere, there's a good chance the pompano will have been frozen. Nothing beats freshly caught fish, fried over an open campfire, something most devoted fishermen love to do. This is an upgraded version of campfire cooking because it uses ingredients most fishermen don't take on a fishing trip.

---

2 medium-size pompano, filleted
salt and freshly ground pepper to taste
3 to 4 tbsp butter
3 to 4 tbsp olive oil
1 cup dry white wine or dry vermouth
3 tbsp freshly chopped tarragon or 1 tbsp dried tarragon
freshly chopped parsley to garnish

Season fillets on both sides with salt and pepper. Melt butter in large skillet over high heat. Add olive oil. Lower heat and place fillets in skillet in single layer, skin side up. (If skillet is not large enough, cook only 2 fillets at a time.) Cook 3 to 4 minutes until lightly browned. Turn with spatula and cook about 5 minutes or until fish flakes easily. Remove to warm serving platter. Pour wine into skillet and deglaze pan. Cook over high heat until reduced by about one-third. Stir in tarragon and pour over fish. Garnish with chopped parsley.

Simple Boiled Shrimp

Shrimp are found in abundance in the Gulf of Mexico and along the Atlantic coastline as far north as North Carolina. Along the coast, where fishermen bring in their catch, you can find many unpretentious restaurants where fresh, delicious shrimp are cooked to order. The number of ways shrimp can be cooked is almost endless. But nothing tastes better than simple, plain, boiled shrimp, served hot or cold with hot spicy cocktail sauce. There is only one trick to cooking shrimp properly — don't overcook them.

Serious shrimp-eaters can eat $1/2$ lb or more shrimp cooked this way. Rinse in cold water and place in large saucepan. Cover with cold water and add seafood seasoning and lemon. Cover pan, but not tightly. Bring water to a rolling boil while you watch. Ignore the old proverb about a watched pot never boiling. As soon as water boils, push pot cover firmly in place so steam can't escape. Take covered pot to sink and slide cover open just enough to pour out water. Be very careful. The steam is HOT! Cover pot tightly again and set aside 10 minutes while shrimp finish cooking in steam trapped in saucepan. Serve hot, cold, or room temperature with cocktail sauce.

If you want to be fancy, peel and devein shrimp before serving. However, it's more fun, and less work for you, if you place shrimp in a large bowl so guests can help themselves and peel their own shrimp, provided of course, you supply lots of napkins.

Broiled Shad Roe

The first shad roe of the season is likely to come from northern Florida or Georgia in January and is much sought after by those familiar with its wondrous flavor. Whenever I think of shad roe, I think of a very special boss I had many years ago. Rex Stout was the creator of the great gourmet detective Nero Wolf. It was through "them" (the character of Nero Wolf often was hard to distinguish from Rex Stout) that I first became dimly aware of the difference between food for survival and really good cooking. Shad Roe was one of "their" favorite foods.

---

2 pair shad roe, carefully washed and trimmed
4 tbsp melted butter, or more as needed
minced shallots, freshly ground pepper, and freshly snipped herbs
such as chervil, tarragon, dill, and/or parsley
8 strips cooked bacon, lemon wedges, and additional melted
butter, if desired, to serve

Place shad roe in single layer in deep skillet or wide saucepan. Cover with lightly salted ice water and let stand about 10 minutes. Simmer gently 5 minutes or until firm. Divide each pair in half and transfer to broiler pan with slotted spatula. Brush generously with melted butter and broil until lightly browned. Turn over carefully, brush with butter, and sprinkle with shallots, pepper, and herbs. Cook until browned on second side. Serve with strips of bacon, lemon wedges, and melted butter.

Southern Collard Greens

Collard greens are a member of the cabbage family and about as southern as you can get in the food department. Chances are you'll have difficulty finding them in other parts of the country except, of course, in a soul food restaurant. Traditionally, collard greens are seasoned with bacon drippings. If bacon drippings are something you don't eat any more, you probably can substitute butter or margarine.

---

1 ham hock
3 bunches collard greens
4 cups liquid from cooked ham hock or chicken stock
4 tbsp bacon drippings, butter or margarine
1/2 tsp sugar or to taste
freshly ground pepper to taste

Place ham hock in saucepan, add enough water to cover, bring to a boil, reduce heat, cover, and simmer 2 hours or until almost tender. Set aside with liquid. Wash greens thoroughly, trim stems, and discard any wilted leaves. Place in large saucepan and add ham hock and 4 cups reserved cooking liquid. Bring to a boil, reduce heat, cover, and cook 30 minutes. Add remaining ingredients and toss greens. Cover and cook until greens are very tender. Adjust seasoning. Remove ham hock and dice meat. Drain greens and add diced ham.

Okra and Tomatoes

About the only time most northerners come into close contact with okra is when they find it in gumbo. Creole dishes often use okra as both a thickening agent and a vegetable. The problem with okra is that when it is overcooked, it takes on a mucilaginous consistency that can be very unpleasant. But young, crisp okra, properly cooked, is delicious, particularly when served over rice or grits.

---

2 to 3 tbsp butter
1 small onion, chopped
1 lb baby okra, stems trimmed
1 clove garlic, minced
1 can (16 oz) stewed tomatoes, mashed
$1/2$ tsp sugar
$1/4$ tsp oregano
salt and freshly ground pepper to taste
cooked rice or grits to serve

Melt butter in saucepan and sauté onion until transparent. Add okra and cook 5 minutes. Add garlic and cook 2 minutes. Add remaining ingredients, stir gently, cover, and cook over low heat about 20 minutes or until okra is just tender. Serve over rice or grits.

Black-Eyed Peas and Ham Hocks

The term "soul food" came into being in the 1960s. It's used to describe dishes like this, created by slaves who, in desperation, learned how to feed their families with leftover food and anything else edible they could find. Soul food provides a rich heritage of family and survival, as well as evidence of the cooking talents and creativity of the black population of the early rural South.

2 lb smoked ham hocks
1 pkg (16 oz) dried black-eyed peas
1 onion, chopped
2 stalks celery, chopped
2 dried hot red chili peppers, crumbled
freshly ground black pepper
(serves 8)

Place ham hocks in large saucepan, add enough water to cover, bring to a boil, reduce heat, cover, and simmer 2 hours or until almost tender. Meanwhile, place peas and 6 cups water in separate large saucepan. Bring to a boil and cook 3 minutes. Cover and let stand 1 hour. Drain peas and add to cooked ham hocks with remaining ingredients. Cover and simmer 45 minutes or until peas are tender. Peas should absorb most of liquid. Add additional water during cooking if necessary, or remove pot cover and cook uncovered if there is too much liquid. Remove ham hocks, dice meat, and stir into peas.

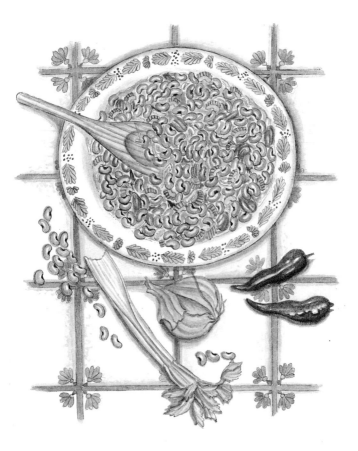

Corn Fritters

Thomas Jefferson unquestionably is the president who influenced food and eating in America more than any other chief executive. Corn appeared in many forms on his table at Monticello. Recipes like Corn Fritters and Corn Pudding are traditional to southern cooking and are also considered soul food. These Corn Fritters are the perfect accompaniment to ham.

---

1 cup all-purpose flour
1 tsp baking powder
2 cups whole-kernel corn, fresh, frozen and thawed, or canned and drained
2 eggs, separated
¹/₂ cup milk
salt and freshly ground pepper to taste
butter and vegetable oil for cooking
honey to serve (optional)

Place flour in bowl, stir in baking powder, add corn, and stir. Beat egg yolks in separate bowl, add milk, stir into corn mixture, and season to taste. Beat egg whites and fold into corn mixture. Heat equal amounts of butter and oil in skillet until very hot. Drop batter by tablespoonfuls into skillet and cook about 4 minutes or until golden. Turn with spatula and cook until golden on second side. Drain on paper towels and serve hot with honey.

Bourbon Sweet Potato Casserole

The deep orange sweet potatoes grown in the South are usually called yams to distinguish them from the pale yellow sweet potatoes grown in the North. Even though they're called yams, they're not yams — they're orange sweet potatoes. Yams belong to an entirely different botanical family. But, no matter what they're called, orange sweet potatoes have the best flavor. Use them for this delicious casserole.

---

6 medium-size orange sweet potatoes, boiled
4 tbsp butter
4 tbsp brown sugar
1/4 tsp cinnamon
1/4 tsp nutmeg
salt to taste
4 to 6 tbsp bourbon
finely chopped walnuts or pecans
(serves 6 to 8)

Preheat oven to 375°F. Butter 2-quart casserole. Peel and mash potatoes. Place in bowl and stir in butter, sugar, and seasonings. Beat in bourbon and spoon into prepared casserole dish. Scatter chopped nuts on top and bake about 30 minutes.

This dish can be made for the children by substituting orange juice for bourbon and topping casserole with marshmallows during last 10 minutes of baking.

Watermelon Rind Pickles

Watermelons always remind me of my years at summer camp. Periodically there would be an announcement that a generous parent had provided a watermelon treat for the camp. All the other campers were thrilled, but the only thing I liked about watermelon was the inevitable "seed spitting" contest. The fact that I had no desire to eat watermelon was viewed as distinctly weird. In due course I discovered Watermelon Rind Pickles, which I really like, although I'm still willing to leave fresh watermelon to those who appreciate it more than I do.

---

2 tbsp salt
6 to 7 cups watermelon rind, green skin and
pink flesh removed, cut into 1-inch pieces
5 cups sugar
2 cups cider vinegar
bouquet garni of:
1 or 2 tbsp each whole cloves and whole allspice;
1 cinnamon stick, broken;
1 lemon, quartered

Place salt and 4 cups water in saucepan. Add watermelon and soak overnight. Drain, rinse, cover with fresh water, simmer 10 minutes, and drain. Place remaining ingredients and 4 cups water in separate saucepan. Boil 5 minutes. Add rind to saucepan, and cook 45 minutes or until transparent. Discard *bouquet garni* and pack watermelon and liquid in hot sterilized jars. Process 20 minutes in boiling-water bath.

Guava Sauce

Few, if any, fresh guavas are imported by the U.S. And, since guavas are a small crop, they're not always easy to find. It's easier to find guava jelly and guava paste and they're worth buying. Use them as you would other jellies or jams. The taste is unique. Fortunately my brother-in-law makes guava jelly occasionally and sends us some. But jelly can be very difficult to make because guavas tend to be temperamental and, in spite of their pectin content, don't always cooperate and set properly. On the other hand, Guava Sauce is easy to make and a few spoonfuls are delicious with poultry and pork, served over ice cream, or stirred into softened cream cheese.

---

2 lbs ripe guavas, ends trimmed and diced
1 cup sherry, sweet or dry
1 cup sugar, or to taste
lemon or lime juice to taste
(makes about 3 cups)

Place ingredients in saucepan and bring to a boil. Reduce heat and simmer 25 minutes or until guavas are soft. Purée in food processor or blender and press through non-metal sieve. Cover and store in refrigerator. Serve hot or cold.

Mississippi Mud Pie

I can't locate the origin of this pie, or find out how it got its name. Evidently no one seems to know. Curiously, there are two entirely different recipes that have the same name. One recipe is a chocolate crumb crust filled with ice cream, covered with chocolate sauce or glaze, and topped with whipped cream. The recipe below takes a bit more work — but not much. Both versions are delicious.

---

pastry for single crust 9-inch pie
4 oz (4 squares) semisweet chocolate
1/2 cup butter
3 eggs
3 tbsp light corn syrup
3/4 cup sugar
I tsp vanilla or almond extract
pinch of salt (optional)
vanilla ice cream, coffee ice cream, or
flavored whipped cream to serve
(serves 6 to 8)

Preheat oven to 350°F. Line 9-inch pie plate with pastry. Melt chocolate and butter in heavy saucepan over moderate heat. Beat eggs and stir in corn syrup, sugar, vanilla, and salt. Stir into chocolate mixture slowly, stirring constantly, and pour into pastry-lined pie plate. Bake about 35 minutes or until set but soft inside. Serve warm with ice cream or whipped cream.

Peach Upside-Down Cake

Peaches are either "freestone" or "clingstone." The clingstones usually end up in cans; the freestones are the peaches sold fresh. They are at their best in June, July, and August. When fresh peaches are in season, use them to make this delicious cake and the dessert that follows.

---

4 tbsp butter plus 5 $1/3$ tbsp butter
$1/2$ cup firmly packed brown sugar plus
I cup firmly packed brown sugar
$1/2$ tsp cinnamon
4 firm, fresh peaches, blanched, peeled, pitted, and sliced
2 eggs
I $1/2$ cups cake flour
I $1/2$ tsp each baking powder and ginger
$1/2$ tsp each nutmeg and salt
I tbsp grated orange peel
$1/2$ cup milk
flavored whipped cream to serve (optional)
(serves 8)

Preheat oven to 350°F. Melt 4 tbsp butter in 9-inch round cake pan. Stir in $1/2$ cup brown sugar. Add cinnamon, stir, and spread over bottom of cake pan. Arrange sliced peaches over mixture. Cream 5 $1/3$ tbsp butter in mixing bowl. Add I cup brown sugar and beat well. Beat in eggs, I at a time. Sift next 5 ingredients together. Stir in orange peel and add to bowl alternately with milk. Beat until well combined. Pour batter over peaches and spread evenly. Bake about 40 minutes or until toothpick comes out clean. Cool in pan on wire rack 2 minutes.

Run knife gently around sides of pan. Place warm serving plate over pan, hold tightly together, and invert. Let stand 4 minutes and carefully remove pan from cake. Serve warm or cold with whipped cream.

Quick Georgia Peach Treat

Fresh peaches and ice cream make a wonderful dessert and a liqueur topping makes it even more festive.

---

fresh peaches
coffee ice cream
fresh blueberries
coffee liqueur or coffee syrup
fresh mint leaves to garnish

For each portion, blanch 1 peach, peel, cut in half, and remove pit. Arrange peach halves in individual serving dishes, rounded side down. Place scoop of ice cream in each peach half. Scatter blueberries over ice cream and and pour 2 or 3 tbsp coffee liqueur on top. Garnish with mint leaves and serve immediately.

Broiled Grapefruit

Those of us who live in the North, and are lucky enough to have a patch of land on which we can grow vegetables, are inordinately proud of our ability to go into the garden and pick fresh tomatoes and a few springs of basil during the summer months. But if you live in parts of the South, there are many months of the year when you can pick grapefruit, oranges, or other citrus fruit from a tree in your own yard. Chilled grapefruit, delicious as it is, is pretty standard fare. But Broiled Grapefruit is somewhat unusual. Serve it for breakfast or dessert when grapefruit is at its best, from December through June.

$1/2$ grapefruit
brown sugar or honey
butter
orange-flavored brandy
mint leaves and/or fresh strawberry to garnish
(serves I)

Section grapefruit half so it will be easy to eat. Place in flameproof baking dish, cut side up. Sprinkle generously with sugar and dot with butter. Broil about 5 inches from source of heat until sugar begins to caramelize and fruit is thoroughly heated. Sprinkle with brandy. Garnish with mint leaves and/or strawberry and serve hot.

New Orleans Pralines

Pralines are sold everywhere in New Orleans. If you're there, you can arrange to ship some home. If you're not there, and have become addicted, you can order them by mail or make them yourself. Someone once told me if you break a praline in half, all the calories will fall out! I wish I could believe it.

---

4 tbsp sweet butter
I cup firmly packed light brown sugar
I cup granulated sugar
I cup light cream
I cup coarsely chopped pecans
I tbsp vanilla
(makes about 30 candies)

Lightly grease 2 baking sheets. Melt butter in large heavy saucepan. Add sugars and cream and cook over moderate heat, stirring constantly with long-handled wooden spoon, until sugar is completely dissolved. Bring to a boil, reduce heat, and cook, without stirring, until mixture reaches soft ball stage (240°F on candy thermometer). Remove from heat and stir in pecans and vanilla. Beat just until mixture begins to thicken. Drop by heaping tablespoonfuls onto baking sheets. Each candy should be about $1/2$-inch thick and 2-inches around. Remove from baking sheets with greased spatula when cool. Store in airtight container.

Index